Anthony Battaglia

Finding God; Between the Lines

Anthony Battaglia

First Edition

ISBN: [979-8-XXXXX-XXX-X]

Printed in [United States of America]

Publisher: Publishing Your Dreams

For permissions requests or inquiries, contact the author at [email or website].

Stories. Some inspire us to do great things. Others stir up deep thoughts or questions. The good ones touch our very soul, eliciting emotions that we didn't know we even had or had somehow lost along the way. They leave us yearning for more, or better yet, make us look within.

Each of us have our own unique story. Whether you think your story is boring or tragic, or maybe so unbelievable that not even Hollywood would write it, it is YOURS. And what is a story if it is not shared? Can you imagine a world where there was no Harry Potter or Rudolph the Red Nosed Reindeer? Or better yet, no Frozen? The question of whether or not you wanted to build a snowman would never be followed by an endless tune stuck in your head for hours.

Your story is unique because God made you unique. Crafted in His own image, but shaped by the love He shares with you as His beloved child. A love not meant to stay hidden, but shared. He is proud of you, whether you allow yourself to believe it or not, and like any Father proud of their child, He wants to hold you up for everyone to see.

Yet sometimes we get in our own way don't we? The stresses of everyday life cloud our thoughts and make it hard to see where we should take our next step, let alone even think about why our story is even important to talk about.

This book is a collection of parables. Stories designed to help you reflect on who God is and how you fit into His plans. But these aren't the parables you grew up with. They are a collection of new and original stories drawn from the heart, my heart, and shared with you.

Some you may find boring or downright confusing. Some clever, but maybe a little distant. That's okay, we all relate to stories differently and have our own perspective. My hope is that you just find one that strikes a chord in your heart. One that elicits an emotion that you may have bottled up for years. One that provides an opening in your heart for God so that you may see Him as your loving Father.

Contents

"Trust in the Lord with all your heart and lean not on your own understanding; in all your ways submit to Him and He will make your paths straight."
~Proverbs 3:5-6

My story with God may be similar to a lot of you. I grew up going to Sunday School. I read the bible and knew who Jesus was along with some of the stories, and like many of you even questioned how all of those animals fit on that ark. I checked off the boxes and made sure I followed the rules to get into heaven.

It wasn't until later on in life that I realized I was missing the point entirely. It wasn't about checking boxes, it was about having a real relationship with the one who knows me better than I know myself.

When I was 31 I thought I had it figured out, achieving the American Dream. I had married the love of my life, had two beautiful kids and a house filled with the different types of animals one might expect from having a science teacher as a wife. On paper it looked great, but something was still missing.

I had always had my fair share of health issues, but it was never anything I couldn't manage. There would be a diagnosis, I'd figure out the next steps, then execute the plan. I considered myself to be pretty smart and would just look at things logically. However, there was an issue still brewing in the darkness with my overall mental health.

Unexplained headaches, emotional outbursts and this feeling like I was losing control. I would come home from work and lock myself in a dark room for hours just to deal with the headaches. When I would emerge I would do everything in my power to control everything to avoid accidentally triggering another headache. It was exhausting and I could see the strain it put on my whole family. Day after day, month after month, no matter what I did I could not stop the spiraling.

Then came November of 2016, the month in the calendar I had previously always looked forward to. Family and friends coming home for the holidays, along with my birthday get together, to catch up and share stories with those in my life. But that get together never came this year. Whether my own perception or reality, I had pushed people away in my effort to solve my health issues.

A false self-emerged, preventing anyone from seeing what was truly happening while at the same time not connecting deeply with the ones I loved. It was at this moment I came face to face with a decision; either seek help, or end my life and the constant pain.

Thankfully, I chose the former. Not out of clarity, but out of absolute desperation as I sat at rock bottom. I did not like being vulnerable or weak. I thought it was my duty as a husband and father to have all the answers, and fighting the stigma that came with mental health issues flew in the face of that. But as I looked at my wife and two young children I knew I had to be better, and that finally led to me reaching out to a professional.

The process went so quickly it's hard to believe. One doctor appointment led to another and before I knew it I was sitting in a therapist's office hearing the words, "You have bipolar." I didn't meet those words with shock or reservation, rather relief that I could finally know what I was battling. While not an easy road, I began to put the pieces back together so I could start feeling whole again, like the real me I had missed for so long.

Relationships improved and I could finally start being the husband and father I always wanted to be. I could set my gaze to what was ahead, not always looking down in shame.

A few months later my world would be turned upside down once again. Not through tragedy but through opportunity. I got an offer from Apple to move 3,000 miles away to California to help with one of their secrete projects. I accepted, not knowing what the role was at all. We then bought a house without even seeing in.

This wasn't intentional, but things just kept falling into place and we just kept saying yes. We found ourselves in a great community with neighbors that immediately stepped in to help us with our needs and embraced us with open arms.

One day, our neighbors The Wilson's stopped by. They told us they had been praying for a family to move into that house with kids the same age as theirs, and invited us to church. Again, we said yes not knowing exactly what we were getting in to. That first day at Covenant Grove is still so vivid in my mind. The smiles, the warm welcomes and a sermon that spoke directly to my soul. It was as if the pastor had been talking with my therapists all along.

At this moment I knew I had found what was missing. The start of a new journey where I knew I would never be alone again. The start of a true relationship with God.

CHAPTER 2

THE LIGHTHOUSE KEEPER

"And God said, "Let there be light..."

~Genesis 1:3

There was once a long stretch of coastline where ships were constantly wrecking. The waters weren't evil—just unpredictable. Fog rolled in without warning, and the rocks were hidden just beneath the surface.

So, the Lighthouse Keeper built a great light on the cliff, and every night, he lit it.

Sailors could see the beam from miles away. It didn't force their ships to turn. It didn't shout commands across the water. It simply stood where it always had, shining steadily, saying without words:

"This way is safe."

Some captains trusted the light and adjusted their course. They made it home.
Others scoffed.

"I know these waters," they said.
Or, "I'll find my own way."

And some ships never made it to shore.

Over time, people began to forget why the lighthouse existed at all. So, the Lighthouse Keeper did something no one expected.

He left the tower.

He came down to the shoreline and boarded the smallest, most fragile boat. He sailed directly into the fog—toward the very ships that were lost.

Through the storm, sailors heard a voice calling from the darkness:

"Follow me. I know these waters. I built the light."

Some recognized the voice and followed it to safety. Others couldn't believe the Keeper would risk himself for them.

But when the storm finally cleared, there was something new on the cliff.

The light was still shining.

Only now, the sailors understood:

The light wasn't there to judge the ships.
It was there because the Keeper loved them—and refused to give up on any who were lost.

●●●

God doesn't force direction; He provides light. And when we're lost, He comes looking for us.

This parable teaches that true guidance is rooted in love, not control.

The lighthouse does not force obedience or condemn those who ignore it. It simply remains faithful—steady, visible, and trustworthy. Some respond with humility and are guided safely; others rely on their own confidence and are lost, not because they are punished, but because they refuse the help offered.

The turning point reveals the deeper truth: when guidance alone is not enough, the Keeper enters the danger himself. He does not abandon his post, nor does he demand compliance from afar. He steps into the fog, risking himself to reach those who cannot—or will not—find the way on their own.

The final image reframes everything: the light was never about judgment. It was always about love that refuses to give up, even at great personal cost.

CHAPTER 3

THE CLOCKMAKER

"Restore to me the joy of your salvation and uphold me with
a willing spirit."

~Psalm 51:12

There was once a master clockmaker known throughout the city. His clocks were famous not because they were flashy, but because they kept perfect time. People trusted them with their lives—trains, factories, hospitals.

One day, a young apprentice asked him,
"Why do you care so much about fixing old clocks? Wouldn't it be easier to just build new ones?"

The clockmaker smiled and said nothing.

Years passed. The city grew louder. Faster. More distracted. People stopped maintaining their clocks. Some tried to fix them on their own. Others ignored them entirely.

Soon, clocks everywhere began to fail.

People blamed the clocks.
They blamed time itself.
Some even blamed the clockmaker.

So, the clockmaker did something unexpected.

He opened his workshop doors and invited anyone to bring their broken clocks inside—for free.

But here's the strange part. He didn't just repair them and send them back. He sat with each owner and asked,

"Do you want this clock to tell time... or to be trusted again?"

Some laughed and left. Others stayed.

For those who stayed, the clockmaker did delicate work. He realigned tiny gears. He replaced damaged springs. He cleaned what had been neglected. It took time.

And when the clock was finished, the owner noticed something. The clock now ticked in rhythm with the clockmaker's own master clock.

Not forced.

Not controlled.

Simply aligned.

And the clockmaker said,
"This clock was never broken beyond repair. It just lost connection to the source of time."

•••

God doesn't throw people away; He restores them. He doesn't just fix behavior—He realigns hearts.

This parable teaches that brokenness is often a matter of disconnection, not worthlessness. The clocks fail not because they were badly made, but because they were neglected, misaligned, or repaired apart from the one who understood them. The clockmaker's response is not frustration or replacement, but restoration. He does not rush the process or simply fix surface problems—he tends to what is hidden, small, and essential.

The key moment comes in the question: *Do you want this clock to tell time, or to be trusted again?* Restoration here is about reliability, integrity, and relationship, not mere function. When the clocks are realigned with the master clock, they regain their purpose naturally, without force.

The parable reveals a God who restores people by reconnecting them to the source of life—patiently and personally—rather than discarding them or demanding perfection.

CHAPTER 4

THE GARDENER AND THE WINTER FIELD

"And let us not grow weary of doing good, for in due season we will reap, if we do not give up."

~Galatians 6:9

There was a gardener who owned a wide field on the edge of a village. In the spring and summer, the field was beautiful rows of grain, flowers along the edges, fruit trees heavy with color.

But every winter, the field looked dead.

The soil hardened. The plants withered. The wind stripped the land bare.

Villagers would walk past and say,
"The gardener has abandoned his field."

Some offered advice.

"Plant faster-growing seeds."

"Cover the field so it never feels winter."

"Move on and start somewhere else."

But every morning—even in the cold—the gardener came.

He walked the rows. He checked the soil. He pulled weeds no one else could see. Sometimes, he did nothing at all except stand quietly, hands in his pockets, watching the land.

A child once asked him,

"Why do you keep coming if nothing is growing?"

The gardener replied,

"Because roots grow where eyes can't see."

Spring eventually came.

The field returned—not rushed, not forced—but stronger than before. The harvest was deeper. The soil richer. The plants more resilient to the wind.

And the villagers finally understood:

The field was never abandoned. It was being prepared.

•••

This parable teaches that absence of visible growth does not mean absence of care.

When the field enters winter, it appears lifeless, leading others to assume abandonment or failure.

Their instinct is to rush the process, avoid hardship, or start over entirely.

The gardener, however, understands the deeper work of growth—what matters most is happening underground, beyond immediate sight.

His daily presence, even when nothing seems to change, shows that preparation often looks like stillness.

The field's later strength is not accidental; it is the result of patient tending through a season that could not be skipped.

The parable reminds us that difficult, quiet seasons are not wasted time. They are often the very conditions that make lasting growth possible.

CHAPTER 5

THE BRIDGE BUILDER

"Make me to know your ways, O Lord; teach me your paths."

~Psalm 25:4

There was a village divided by a wide river. The water wasn't violent, but it was deep, cold, and constantly moving.

On one side lived families, work, and daily life. On the other side were fields, rest, and places people went to remember who they were.

Long ago, a master builder constructed a strong bridge between the two sides. It was simple, sturdy, and carefully measured.

At first, everyone used it. But over time, people grew impatient.

"The bridge takes too long," some said.
"I'll build my own crossing," others replied.

So, they did.

Some lashed together planks. Some stacked stones. Some tried to swim across on their own strength.

A few made it. Many didn't.

When their crossings failed, people grew angry. They blamed the river. They blamed the builder. Some even claimed the bridge was never real to begin with.

So the master builder did something unexpected.

He didn't shout instructions from the riverbank. He didn't tear down the broken crossings.

He stood on the bridge.

All day.

Anyone who stepped onto it noticed something strange:

The bridge felt steadier near him. The wind quieter. The fear less sharp.

A traveler once asked,
"Why don't you just force people to use the bridge?"

The builder answered,
"Because love doesn't force trust. It waits for it."

And slowly, people returned—not because they were told to, but because the bridge led somewhere good...and the builder never left it.

•••

God is the one who builds the Way and always stands by our side.

This parable teaches that trust is built through presence, not pressure.

The bridge represents a way that is sound and trustworthy, but not fast or flashy. When people grow impatient, they attempt to create their own solutions. Some succeed briefly; many fail. Their frustration turns outward, blaming circumstances, the builder, or even denying the bridge's existence altogether.

The builder's response reveals the heart of the parable. Rather than forcing compliance or arguing, he chooses presence. By standing on the bridge, he reassures those who are afraid—not with commands, but with companionship. His nearness makes the way feel safer, calmer, and more possible.

The lesson is that love does not compel belief or obedience. It remains faithful, waits patiently, and invites trust to grow naturally.

CHAPTER 6

THE MUSIC TEACHER

"How good and pleasant it is when God's people live together in unity!"

~Psalm 133:1

There was a music teacher known throughout the town. He never advertised. He never chased students.

Instead, he kept his studio door open.

Inside were instruments of every kind—violins, drums, pianos, flutes—each tuned and ready. Soft music often drifted out into the street, not loud enough to interrupt, but clear enough to be noticed.

People walked by every day.

Some paused. Some listened. Some scoffed and said, "If he were any good, he'd force people to hear him."

A few stepped inside.

The teacher never grabbed their hands or told them what to play. He asked one question instead:

"What song are you trying to make?"

Some students played wildly—too fast, too loud, out of rhythm. Others barely touched the keys, afraid of making mistakes.

The teacher didn't shame them. He sat beside them.

Sometimes he played along quietly. Sometimes he adjusted a string or tapped a steady beat on the table. Sometimes he said nothing at all—just listened.

Over time, the students noticed something remarkable.

When they played with him nearby, their music changed—not because they were forced, but because they were aligned.

And when they finally learned to hear his rhythm, the music felt less like effort and more like joy.

The door remained open. Some never entered. Some came and left. Some stayed.

But the teacher never stopped playing.

●●●

God does not force obedience. He invites harmony through the rhythm of love.

This parable teaches that true guidance is invitational, not coercive.

The music teacher does not demand attention, force participation, or control outcomes. Instead, he creates a space that is open, prepared, and welcoming. Those who enter are not corrected through shame or rigid instruction, but through presence and companionship.

Transformation happens not because the students are forced to change, but because they are brought into alignment with a steady, loving rhythm. The teacher listens before he leads, and his quiet nearness reshapes the music naturally.

The open door remains a powerful symbol: relationship is always available but never imposed. Growth comes through willingness and shared presence, not pressure.

CHAPTER 7

WRITTEN IN STONE

"Before I formed you in the womb I knew you, before you were born, I set you apart..."

~Jeremiah 1:5

There was a sculptor who lived at the edge of a city. People knew him for his quiet work and his refusal to rush. One day, a young man brought him a rough stone and said, "Can you make something beautiful out of this?"

The sculptor turned the stone over in his hands for a long time. Then he asked a strange question.

"Do you know what's already inside it?"

The young man laughed.

"It's just a stone."

The sculptor nodded and began his work.

Each day, the young man returned, and each day he grew frustrated.

The sculptor chipped away slowly—sometimes removing large pieces, sometimes just dust. Often, he seemed to do nothing at all except sit quietly, studying the stone.

"Why are you taking so long?" the young man asked.

"You could be finished by now."

The sculptor replied,
"I'm not creating something new. I'm revealing what already exists."

Weeks passed.

At last, the sculptor stepped back.

From the stone emerged a figure—not perfect, not polished smooth, but strong and unmistakably alive. Carved faintly into the base was a name the young man had never told anyone.

"How did you know?" he whispered.

The sculptor said,

"The name was always there. I just removed what wasn't true."

•••

God knows who you truly are and patiently removes what hides it.

This parable teaches that transformation is about uncovering truth, not inventing identity.

The sculptor does not rush or force the process, because he understands that the stone already holds its true form. What looks like delay or inactivity is actually discernment—knowing what to remove and what to preserve.

The most powerful moment is the revealed name. It shows that identity is not something imposed from the outside, but something deeply known and patiently revealed. We are not empty material waiting to be shaped at random—we are already known.

CHAPTER 8

UNLIT CANDLES

"Many are the plans in a person's heart, but it is the Lord's purpose that prevails."

~Proverbs 19:21

There was a candle maker who crafted candles by hand. Each one was shaped carefully, smoothed patiently, and filled with a wick placed exactly at the center.

People came to his shop every day.

Some admired the candles and said,

"These are beautiful. I'll put them on my shelf."

Others carried them through the streets, unlit, careful not to damage them.

A few complained, "What good is a candle if it doesn't shine?"

One evening, a traveler returned with a candle melted, scarred, and misshapen.

"I tried to protect it," the traveler said, embarrassed. "But I finally lit it...and it didn't look the same."

The candle maker smiled.

"Of course, it didn't," he said. "It was never meant to stay untouched."

He held up a new candle and an old, burned one side by side.

"This one," he said, pointing to the perfect candle, "has potential."

Then he pointed to the burned one.

"This one has fulfilled its purpose."

The traveler asked, "But doesn't the flame destroy the candle?"

The maker replied, "No. The flame reveals what the candle was made for."

•••

God does not preserve us, so we remain unchanged. He invites us to burn with purpose.

This parable teaches that purpose is fulfilled through action, not preservation.

The unlit candles remain perfect but unused admired yet ineffective. The traveler's candle, though scarred and altered, has done what it was created to do. The change is not failure; it is faithfulness.

CHAPTER 9

THE LOST BLUEPRINT

"The Lord is merciful and gracious, slow to anger, and abounding
in steadfast love."

~Psalm 103:8

There was a builder who designed a home meant to last generations. Every wall had purpose. Every window was placed for light. Every beam carried weight exactly where it should.

Before construction began, he handed each worker a blueprint.

At first, everyone followed it. But over time, some workers stopped looking at the plans.

"I know how houses work," one said.

"This part slows things down," another argued.

Others lost their blueprints altogether and began guessing.

The house still went up—but cracks appeared. Doors didn't open smoothly. Rooms felt dark even at midday. Some beams strained under loads they were never meant to carry.

When frustration grew, the builder returned to the site.

People expected him to scold them. Instead, he spread the original blueprint on a table and said,

"Nothing is wrong with the house that remembering the design won't heal."

One worker asked, "What if we've already built it wrong?"

The builder replied, "Then we rebuild the parts that matter most."

He stayed—not to tear the house down, but to restore it to what it was always meant to be.

•••

This parable teaches that drift from design leads to strain, but restoration is always possible.

The workers don't fail because they stop working; they fail because they stop referring to the original plan.

Their confidence and shortcuts create something functional on the surface but unstable underneath. The builder's return reveals grace rather than condemnation.

He does not erase the work or shame the workers; he calls them back to the design that always existed. Restoration is not about starting over completely, but about rebuilding what matters most with clarity and care.

When life feels strained or misaligned, the answer is often not more effort, but a return to original purpose.

CHAPTER 10

THE SILENT WELL

"Wait for the Lord; be strong and take heart and wait for the
Lord!"

~Psalm 27:14

There was a village built around an old well. For generations, it had provided water—cool, steady, reliable.

But one summer, the well stopped producing.

People gathered around it, lowering buckets again and again. Nothing came up.

Some said, "The well is empty."

Others said, "It's broken."

A few insisted, "We should dig a new one somewhere else."

But the well keeper did something different.

Each morning, he came early. He cleaned the stones. He checked the ropes. He listened—placing his ear near the opening, waiting.

A child asked him, "Why do you keep coming if there's no water?"

The keeper replied, "Because silence doesn't mean absence."

Weeks passed.

One dawn, as the keeper lowered the bucket, he felt the rope grow heavy. Water surfaced—clearer and colder than before.

The villagers rejoiced and asked, "What changed?"

The keeper smiled and said, "The source was always there. The well just needed time to deepen."

•••

God is present even in the silence, drawing life from depths we haven't yet reached.

This parable teaches that silence is not the same as abandonment.

When the well stops producing, the villagers assume failure and rush to conclusions—empty, broken, no longer worth trusting. Their instinct is to replace what has gone quiet.

The well keeper understands that what sustains life often works beyond immediate visibility. His daily care is not an attempt to force results, but an act of trust.

The water returns not because something new appeared, but because the source had been deepening all along.

CHAPTER 11

TRAVELER IN THE NIGHT

"Walk in obedience to all that the Lord your God has commanded
you, so that you may live and prosper."

~Deuteronomy 5:33

There was a traveler who journeyed across a vast desert at night. The terrain was flat, but the path was hard to see. Every direction looked the same.

Above him shone a single bright star.

The traveler noticed it early in his journey and began using it as his guide. He didn't walk straight toward it—it was too high for that—but he kept it just off his right shoulder as he moved.

Some nights, clouds covered the sky. The traveler stopped and waited.

Other travelers laughed at him.

"Why wait?" they said. "Just walk. Movement is better than standing still."

But the traveler remembered the star.

When the clouds passed, he adjusted his course again.

Days later, he reached an oasis. The water was clear. The ground firm. Shelter stood nearby.

When asked how he found the place, the traveler said, "I didn't chase the star. I let it keep me oriented."

•••

Faith is not chasing certainty, it is staying oriented to what is true, even when the way forward is unclear.

This parable teaches that guidance is not about chasing certainty but maintaining orientation.

Progress without orientation can lead you farther from where you are meant to go.

Waiting is not failure here—it is faithfulness.

CHAPTER 12

DEEP WATER

"Do not worry about anything; instead, pray about everything.
Tell God what you need and thank Him for all He has done."

~Philippians 4:6–7

The teacher replied, "You wouldn't have believed me until you let go."

There was a village beside a wide river. The water was calm near the shore, but deep and powerful toward the center.

A teacher stood at the riverbank each day, inviting people to learn how to cross.

Some stepped in only ankle-deep and said, "This is far enough. I don't need more."

Others waded to their knees, felt the current tug, and hurried back.

"This is dangerous," they warned.

One day, a young learner stepped forward and said, "I want to cross—but I don't know how."

The teacher nodded and led him into the water.

As the river grew deeper, fear filled the boy's chest.

"I can't touch the bottom anymore," he cried.

The teacher said gently, "That is because you were never meant to rely on the bottom."

Then the teacher placed one hand beneath the learner's arm and said, "Stop trying to hold yourself up."

When the learner finally relaxed, he realized something surprising.

He was floating.

The current carried them forward—not chaotically, but steadily—until they reached the far shore.

Shaking, the learner asked, "Why didn't you tell me sooner that you would hold me?"

●●●

Faith begins when we stop trying to hold ourselves up and allow ourselves to be carried.

This parable teaches that true trust begins where self-reliance ends.

Support is already present, but it can only be experienced through letting go.

CHAPTER 13

THE WINDMILL

"Be dressed in readiness, and keep your lamps lit."

~Luke 12:35

There was a farmer who owned a windmill on a wide plain. The mill was meant to grind grain, but only when the wind blew.

When the air was still, the farmer grew anxious.

He pushed the blades by hand. He climbed the tower and pulled ropes. He worked until his arms ached. Still, the mill produced nothing.

An older farmer watched him one evening and said, "That mill was never meant to be powered by your strength."

The younger farmer replied, "But if I don't do something, nothing will happen."

The older farmer smiled.

"Your work is not to create the wind. Your work is to keep the mill ready."

So, the farmer stopped forcing the blades.

He repaired the gears. He oiled the joints. He cleared the stones below.

And when the wind finally came—quietly, without announcement—the mill turned freely, producing more grain than ever before.

•••

Our work is not to create the wind, but to stay ready when it comes.

This parable teaches the difference between control and readiness.

Forcing outcomes often delays fruit, while faithful preparation makes room for it.

I hope you found yourself on a meaningful journey as you read through these parables. I try to find inspiration in the ordinary, everyday moments of life and share them with those who may need encouragement.

As we come to a close, I felt there was no better way to end my first book than to include a few reflections from individuals who have been such an inspiration to me on my journey to God.

Scott Nelson was the pastor at Covenant Grove Church, and one of the first people to greet me when I came through the doors. I credit him for jumpstarting my journey and opening my eyes to what it really meant to know God.

Currently Scott serves as the Associate Superintendent of the Northwest Conference [Church Planting and Leadership Development].

From Scott:

It has been said, "Words create worlds." Words are powerful, and stories shape our lives. God's revelation in the Bible is primarily told through stories, and God's Son is called the "Word."

I have the joy of being Anthony's friend and brother in Christ, and I had the honor to be his pastor for a number of years. Reading through these parables, I am struck at how God is described – as a lighthouse keeper, clock maker, gardener, bridge builder and more. These parables are an invitation to know our Creator in a personal, vulnerable way.

Tragically, most people never experience their Maker this way. Your view of God impacts your entire life – it shapes your life story. God is not distant, angry, or against you.

The Lord loves you, pursues you, and has a plan for you in His Story. I hope these stories can invite you into a deeper relationship with the Author.

Zach Riley is currently the pastor at Radiant Covenant Church and one of the most kind and relatable people you will ever come across. The way he models saying "Yes" to God and embracing whatever opportunities get put in our way will forever be a shining example for me on how I try to live my life every single day.

From Zach:

I first met Anthony Battaglia while visiting Covenant Grove Church to invite those interested to join a church planning team. I shared the true story of a rowdy fan named Steve Davies who was invited to play the second half for a Premier League soccer team, West Ham United. I encouraged listeners not to be spectators in God's story, but participants-for that is what Jesus invites us to be.

After the service, an excited and energetic Anthony came up to me with a hearty, "I am in." In classic Battaglia fashion, he bought a Davies jersey and jumped into the launch team with a joy, vigor, and kindness that still brings a smile to my face. I am deeply grateful that Anthony's story and mine became connected that day.

In Anthony's collection of provocative parables, you will find that you, too, are bring invited to become a participant in the story. These stories invite us to reflect om what it means to join our story to the wonderful story God is writing in our lives.

One clear theme running throughout is the unforced and gentle nature of God's invitational grace. Ponder these parables and consider how you might not just think about God but meet God.

As Anthony writes in his parable "The Lighthouse Keeper":

"When guidance alone is not enough, the Keeper enters the danger himself. He does not abandon his post, nor does he demand compliance from afar. He steps into the fog, risking himself to reach those who cannot-or will not-find the way on their own."

Friends, we do not have to find the way on our own. I am grateful for Anthony's reminder about this vital truth.

Zach Riley